My Shout

Gordon McPherson

My Shout

My Shout
ISBN 978 1 74027 930 7
Copyright © text Gordon McPherson 2015
Cover design: Ari Bickley

First published 2015 by
GINNINDERRA PRESS
PO Box 3461 Port Adelaide 5015 Australia
www.ginninderrapress.com.au

Contents

Adelaide Winter	7
Adult	8
Ancient Airs	9
Bateman's Bay	11
Bifurcation	12
Can't Win	14
Caudillo	15
Chiaroscuro	17
Clichés	19
December Night	21
Desert Pea	23
Eclipse 2002	25
Famille Verte	27
Floodlights at the Walkerville Oval	28
Growing Moon	30
Heisenberg's Uncertainty Principle	31
How Fundamentalists Explain Conception	33
Infrared Hunters (A Species Radiates)	35
Julia's Spin Doctor	36
Junior Soccer Coach	38
Karma	41
Lascaux	43
Like You	45
Midday Walk	46
Muse of Sunsets	47
Neo Con	49
New Jerusalem	51
Open Cut	52
oral	53
Parallel Rider	55

Plato's Horses – From *Phaedrus*	57
Psychotoxic	59
Raku	60
Reliquary	62
Snake	64
Soccer Balls	66
Supermen	68
The Elite	71
Time	72
Too Lazy	74
Trance	75
Voyagers in the Tea Tree Gully Library	76
Willow	78
Winter Black	80
Witchcraft	82

Adelaide Winter

We are clutched by a species of hunger,
(Hunger unassuming, Australian),
We hurried citizens as we wander
Among the pale eddies of wind which run

Through the tattered rags of our daily time,
Treading so remotely and so removed.
A throng gusted and harrowed, we remind
Of Tartarus, yet loose among the day's noon.

We behold your gaunt memorial buildings,
Sorrowful Stonehenges and obelisks,
Your glass-bound catacombs, uplifted things,
High raised, hi-tech, an ideologue's fist.

Peeping listlessly at the third world's shore,
Inert to what force moves its history,
Except to the lathering click of keyboards
And the buzz of light-speed mediocrity,

You drowse beyond the sting of any dream,
No sooth nor seer divining any doubt,
And your blood flows with usurer's ease
To close accounts, to kick the tenants out.

Adult

I am startled
At the laughter of children
And startled too
At my surprise.
I note their behaviour
As some strange flower
Abounding on the hillsides
And pulling down
A nirvana of primary hues.

Their directness and incapacity
To defer or deform their emotions,
Their inborn genius for wholeness,
Startles me.

Even when some superego
Baubles them like ornaments
And in the wearing
Usurps their wealth,
Or where some zealot
Knifes them up with sin,
They remain so remote
From the contempt of adults.

And so remote must I be
From their mystic diamond bodies
That my own psychic shape
Makes its noises
And reasserts its startled form.

Ancient Airs

To sing
After three hundred decades
Of what can never be new again,
What other music but yours, Respighi,
Would the Muse employ, to give voice
In lyrical despair to the lichen
On those resounding forms
Of ancient stone,
In ancient airs?

In the tiny Italian peninsula
Where the greatest and the least,
From the Antonines to the *contadini*,
Have all left their stamp,
The Fascists rest on empty forms,
For swollen with an intensity
Unfocused on all but resignation,
They perceive through the fanatic's haze
The melancholic exhaustion
Of their history.

They know, too, in the cities,
With their bare plainsong,
Of the mass of antiquity, yet still
They incant, calling to the empty cycles
Of the world in vain harmonies.

Renewal will not come.
Not from the mantra
Of renovated mythology,
Not from the arid blues
Of common sense,
Not from the streetwise
Cant of the corporates,
Not from the ecclesiastical refrain,
Nor even from Garibaldi's
Battle cries, whose generous red
Has by now coagulated
Into Mussolini's Black Bands.
And it is Il Duce
Who commands Respighi
To sing.

Bateman's Bay

The moon over Bateman's Bay entices
The shoreline with a gentle metrical hint
And I the romantic look upon
The blank lines and do not fill them
With broken hills or the melancholy
Relics of the tombs of Celtic warriors,
Nor their helms nor their steeds and retainers.

There are no beasts, no surreal images
Made solid by the waves. There is nothing
But rocks and water and moon radiance,
A bare-boned trinity for the poet.

But no small matter is it, to include
My frugal vision in this, for these three
Elements abolish the sense of time,
And echo with twenty billion years
Of creation and now resound more with
Each differing human remembrance.

Bifurcation

In that intense present,
their talk meandered from
one barbed-wire obligation
of study to another,
the learning log,
the art galleries,
and the official website,
all in a language
disjointed from ordinary sense,
perhaps to hide its unease
with actual construction,
and it never-ended
from the pile of folders
to the kitchen,
through to coffee
and breakfast,
all the way to the driveway
and the open car door.

Niece, all very cazh,
had taken her cup
and as my wife swung
the car away,
I glimpsed,
through two surfaces of glass
one smiling farewell
of a face
and her caffeine shot,
and I suddenly felt
as if an ice sheet,

quietly, distantly
shedding its children,
had made an unalterable split
where the future
secedes from the present.

So all would now
be different
as she rode off
into her unknown
and I remained secure
upon the uncertainties
of what had been left behind.

Can't Win

Granddad, in cap,
shorts and hearing aid,
quietly watches the game
in child-free ennui,
but Miss Royally Raised Brow
approaches him
and asks,
will you come
to my play tonight?
please, please, she sings.

And Granddad says,
Ask Nana.
I've already asked Nana
and she told me to come here
and ask you, she intones,
lingering like a spell
on her last word.

Then circling with her feet,
she scuffs the ground,
flicks the folds
of her fairy costume
and retires from Granddad's
seasoned evasions,
walking through the gates
to find Nana
out on the oval.

Second Front soon.

Caudillo

Franco's face
was on the Spanish coins,
a dull, avuncular
ten-peseta profile
of harmless appeal,
the youthful outlines
having long sagged
with siestas and a full stomach
of satisfying atrocities
and with poetic daydreams
of his monument,
an aroused and vengeful cross,
marking the tomb
of multitudes who would never
roll back the stone
and stand in the light
of their own history.

There was no kinship
in his poetry of dread,
merely a lifeless fluid
strafed in Rebel graffiti
along the refugee roads
or smashed in single-sided
Rorschach blots
of structural terror
under the anonymous ground,
so much resembling
in its scattered shreds
that modern art
his resurrected Spain
so despised,
and so much
the currency of his time.

Chiaroscuro

The voices,
Assaulting and stalking, from everywhere
They come, those voices of the media,
Bobbing up, solarised with the
Buoyancy of a never-ending morning.

They shine in with shafts
Of brightly buttered sunlight,
They bugle in the joyful yellows
Of a bouncing karaoke ball, brimming
With orchestrated songbirds,
And their world, flattened
By the broadness of their brush,
Swirls all things into their
Cartoon rainbow.
The shock jock, archangel
Of compliance, stands guard
Over this cage-bred battery optimism,
Unquestioned and unassailable,

But I still nurse my own voice
Of well guarded melancholy
and savour the passing of day,
Celebrating the exodus
Of those adolescent raptures.
I am attuned instead to the
Syncopated score of dusk
And make my confession
To the swing of the lunar mood.

And although their newly minted grins
And their treasury smiles
Are the small change of our epoch,
Yet I nourish my ambiguous slothful grey
And underground blacks,
My sneaking recessionary defence,
My subversive idleness.

In their rationality,
They banish doubt,
But I, doubtful, have reason.

Clichés

He wears his clichés,
he reaches out every morning
and puts them on,
his trying-to-look-younger shirt
and the same old trousers
with the expanding belt line,
no too newly bright blue jeans
for him
and odd socks probably
and the pullover,
obviously trying
to achieve a younger look
but avoiding the roughneck denim
of a Led Zeppelin youth
and he combs his clichéd thinning hair
and checks the dents and scratches
on his dentition
and he mooches along,
listening to their faraway opinions,
their little clicking wheels
ticking off the answer,
a sixty-year-old platitude.

And when he goes to bed,
he hears his arteries pump
and wonders about
the clichéd cardiac,
or the oh-so-predictable
blood sugar levels
and sleeps the inevitable sleep,
with the inevitable harmless dreams
and no one would suspect
that under this mound
of unoriginality
he plots and ponders
on how to defeat Alexander,
or how to burn down sacred buildings,
or how to assassinate the great ones,
and after all that
remain immune
from prosecution.

December Night

On a green cold
December night,
in a summer freeze
and smoking
with young love's grief,
I rode pillion,
green, cold, away, homeward,
the clutch of acceleration
pulling at my hands,
the memory
pulling at the warmth,
the calculated warmth,
of her rejection.

In the ignorance
of young love,
unadmitted young love,
through the frozen heart
of arrogance,
for fear of being
without defence,
refusing that love's
vulnerable harmonies,
I rode pillion
with self-reproach,
the first, the newest,
the most painful
to repel,
because deserved.

That green cold
December night
still enquires with
unanswerable naivety
of my calculated rejection
as I ride pillion
with that memory
of her calculated warmth,
the clutch of acceleration
pulling at my years.

Desert Pea

Like old men
At second sight,
With fertile bud
Of silken black,
They have seen
The drifting crux
And their sightlessness
Still penetrates
The weathered day
And cobalt night.
Fusion red,
A democracy of fire,
Each one sits crowned
Upon the newborn head
Of the solar year,
Wise as revolution,
Wise as Orc.
If old men burnt so,
Popes would turn in fear
And presidents fend off
Imagined blows.
If women so enflamed,
They'd scorch the hands
That work their ruin,
Their infibulation.
And children,
Brandishing so the
Strength of patience,
The strength of a flower,

With arational logic
Would dismiss the hordes
Of learning,
Like squealing angels
From the head of a pin.

Eclipse 2002

Among the brightly populated hills,
How brilliantly
The night surrounds now
Sappho's wandering moon.
How she wends,
How she instils
A winding stillness,
How she holds up the black sky,
How her full form litters
The unlettered waves
And her trailing dress,
Along the silvery waters,
In the starry ways,
The celestial stairway,
Reflects her path,
Her silvered guesses,
And thus she offers consolation
For the soughing of our desires,
The sea sounded
Mortal sighs.

Having spread her blessings,
The assassin
Now assuages the trauma
Of her assault,
Salving our memory
Of the murdered Sun
And of the dreadful suspension
Of the light,
Where, in that brief silence,

Half a hundred
Diamond skulls
Illuminated her smoking necklace
On the Ceduna shore.

Famille Verte

Green are the hammers
Of celestial creation,
The tormented oxygen green
At the thunder's heart,
Hand on heaven and earth.

Green is the spacious
Planetary breath.

Green is the grey-green rind
Of the distant ocean,
Seeming to rise up.

Green is a wealth of coin,
Swirling in the tree's crown.

Green is the china vessel
Of lustrous deep and
Coolly waxen light.

And green is in gross matter,
Solid with synthetic things
Coiled green around
The ego's throne.

And malefic is the green
And corrupt is the green
Of profound dissolution,
A hazy down of feasting spores.

And poison is the green,
The sullen green
Of the human heart
And its synthetic grin.

Floodlights at the Walkerville Oval

Not quite as warlike
as a Martian fighting machine
and monopod,
they peer down bifocally
from their impassively bright
ice-mint blue eyes
and borrow some
of the Earth's
splendid dusk
yet outstare
its parochial glow.

They perceive
from their impossible
elongations,
with their metallic biology
and their stalking legs,
the treks of the children,
their density of purpose
and their limbs ignoring
the decencies
in their democracy of space.

They hum in ultrasound,
a symphonic chorus
of interstellar insects
jamming with reality,
calling maybe to their allies
at the Exmouth station
of looming daddy-long-legs
that weave spookily
their spidery surveillance
of the entire universe,
or maybe they tweet
in refined gibberish,
hashtags available only
to the young.

And possibly, like great
otherworldly mothers,
each one selects
its offspring
from the children,
as they hurry on by,
busy with the earnest
doings of their eternity
and the punctuation of their
timeless days,
for these creatures
aren't at rest,
immobile as they seem.

Growing Moon

Our talk wandered, underground, random,
In that faraway night. It was a long
Obsessive walk, past the sleeping doors
And windows, under each streetlight, held up
Like beads, and on and on to no resolution –
A high moon, a wedding whiteness of clouds,
Stars, and a liquorice-deep sky. A tense
And young man wretchedness time it was
As spring laughingly withdrew its promise.

And surely there were no inhabitants
Lazing under the moonlight, there were no
Conversations on verandas and in
Gardens, no greetings from the night club crowds
And no signs of another life surfacing
Like a whale, immersing in its surge my
Tiny miseries. And though I know it not
To be so, the moon herself, large as a
Human face, danced ahead and dances now,
To embroider a truth with my memories.

Heisenberg's Uncertainty Principle

hey hi
                         high eyes
hi zen
                                zenburger prinzip
            high sent ounce
            ertainment
            answer taint
            dainty prinzip
sipsipple
sir tame tee
hue zen borough
                          burg burgers of medieval Russia
                               prinz eugen
un cert   ampersand

and absurd   unsort

      ain't ee prinzipal
                     heisenburg's ain't cert ain't he
      führer prinzip
                     for sure and ampersand
                     dissert   station
                     prints a pal
                     prince a

zenburg highs a print's pal
unser taints he
pincer

heisen burr rough is
                uncertainly prinzip
hay cyborg sun
                sunsmart intensity
                führerprinzip!

inselberg zen shirt
                hy borg sum prinzip
                        twenty fin zip
                                  one score pules of baby
inselberg sent shirt
twenty fin zip pule

heysen's unburden shitty
                        prints a nipple

                        hi singer zooms hunt
                        auntie prinks a pull.

By Gawgodowngowdongorbonniedoon
MacmixPhursealsonperson

How Fundamentalists Explain Conception

The father and mother's gametes,
shall they combine
through the sinful genitive organs,
but only in a holy marital state,
after the necessary lamentations.

Then may the chromosomes
miracle themselves together,
and verily may the soul be inserted,
along with original sin,
that old serpent.

Lo, then each unto each other
shall they share themselves out
but not each with the same,
for they shall not.

And may they pull themselves away,
until twofold in number they be.

Behold, as they runneth to the opposite
ends of their cells, God maketh miracles
in them and one cell becometh now two,
and the chromosomes swimmeth about,
according to God's instructions,
unto the end of their appointed time.

And then lineth they up, the chromosomes,
and verily, may their heads be even,
and raceth they away and splitteth themselves
asunder in halves and maketh they then
four daughter cells.

For it cometh to pass
that the Y chromosome shall maketh of them
male or female thus saith the Lord,
and no other, unless original sin
hath already begun
its iniquities.

And then God shall so wield it
that the daughter cells
shall race yet again towards each other,
for lo, the embryo be now made
of diploid numbers and then shall they
double up for nine months,
according to the will of the Lord,
to make a perfect, but still sinful, baby
but only in a loving and sanctified marriage
between male and female
made He them.

For the manual on the miracle of birthing,
but only with miracling and birth trauma,
visit you our website intelligentdesign.org
and download you our pdf.

Infrared Hunters (A Species Radiates)

Their skin is darker than the bleak ores
At the heart of the earth
And crowded with the density
Of melanin, so blue-black,
So mirrored with sweat, it shines
Like the motion of sea beasts,
As the muscles slide like ebony,
Sinuous as volcanic glass.

Lean as their high pointing spears,
Attenuated, made to aim
Away the toxic light,
The new hunters stand humanly grouped,
Bonded by intelligence
And knowledge of time,
Conjoined by purposive behaviour.

They pick their way like storks
Through the superheated world
And feed on the weakened creatures there.
Easy prey, these termites
Who fall gasping
Under the light's heaviness,
Easy prey, these with the pale tender hides.

Their hungry spears and arrows
Engorge themselves
On that strange red blood,
And bring back a feast of alien meat
To their bleak blue camp.

Julia's Spin Doctor

The challenge of the red hair
Was ably met by the background
Of muted blue
And of the twin Australian flags.

Her open jacket hung
In fashionably casual lines,
Its dark hue setting off the sleeves,
Which, of a subdued brown,
Gave an overall and necessary
Slimming effect
And suggested a sombre dignity
So suited for the occasion.

Her face was well accessorised,
The glasses being slightly
Less than moonlike
And slightly more generous
Than those tight little lenses
Most commonly worn these days.

Her make-up responded perfectly
To the demands of publicity,
Giving a mature appearance,
Yet somehow youthful
And highlighting
Her difficult features
In a most sophisticated way.

Julia's voice, never her strong point,
Was measured
And free from that political stridency
Of recent memory,
All signs of recrimination
Being firmly restrained
By our spin doctor's art.

Her almost gracious speech
Was a final ornament
To a long career,
Now conclusively ended
And her last formal appearance
Was happily free from
The weakness of her sex,
Those self-piteous sobs
On mainstream media.

Junior Soccer Coach

I want the balls placed here,
not kicked here,
as soon as you've shot,
you turn and tackle,
but go through the poles,
there's no short cuts,

Phil, you've got to help, keep going,
what are we going to get? Goals!
It's all about getting goals,
are you listening?

Nathan, you've got a job to do,
no short cuts,
it's through the poles,
you go through the poles,

Max, you've got to stop Timmy,
Timmy's scored,
Anthony, back here, Clive,
I just said, go,

Tyson, Tyson,
you've got to stop Rickie,
back in your shape,
give me a wall pass,
do we understand,
we know what a wall pass is?
Right back to him,

Looks like Timmy's
getting another goal,
Nathan, stop Amie,
Anthony, you've got
a job to do, Harry, no no no no!
Through the poles,
why did you go out wide, Clive?

Phil, you've got to keep going,
why pick a ball up?
Kick it, they're all around,
no, not that way,
who wants to be right wing,
everybody in your shape,
new ball, new ball,
what a shot, Timmy,

Harry, where's your shape,
wall pass, I said wall pass,
we pass it wide, then
we go forward,
Clive, you're the left wing,
out to Mum,
Leo, you're giving them goals,
Tyson, back here,
stop Timmy, yes, I know,
he's scored.

Tyson, back here,
go through the poles,
oh Max, what a shot,
just get to the ball, Rickie,
over here, pass to Amie,
Mum, Mum, to Timmy
Harry, get the goal, no, no,
through the poles,

I've said all along,
through the poles, as soon
as you've shot,
turn back and stop them
but through the poles,
no short cuts.

It's Timmy and he's scored
another goal.
Now who's worn out,
Everyone's worn out? Mum?
Anybody worn out?
Nobody's worn out?
Especially not Timmy?
I thought not.

Karma

It works its wily seesaw way
Through our daily lives;
It's a reverberation, a pattern
Stamped out in stereo,
So unlike that classical mythology
Where just one snip
From those immortal shears
Would deposit you, unstrung, into
The Sorrowful Realm of no posterity.

The son reaped distress for his father,
A hard core of grief, the serpent's tooth
At the heart of filial ingratitude,
And the same rough design,
Like a harsh woodcut,
Now works its symmetry
On the grown son's fatherhood,
Where his own son, as if sprung
From some mystic balance,
Now grips his father
With the same thanklessness.

But the grown son does not recall
His weeping father, nor those generous
Provision so unkindly repaid.
Nor can he see his own unhappiness
As the just visitation of Karma,
And to tell him so would be to invite
Further, more elaborate, woundings.

His kin, made powerless
By discretion,
Inhabit their own Dismal Realm
In the full light of day,
And the impotence
Of their own family mythology
Vetoes any wisdom,
Except the wisely knowing nod
At Karma's uproar.

Lascaux

He might believe it
when he stamps them as illegals,
a divine vision warning him,
no doubt, for no other source
could have been available
to provide such an imprimatur,
such a detailed nimbus
of enlightenment,
to him or the rest of his party.

Or he might disbelieve it
when, along with the chorus,
he tags them as *verboten*,
but maybe his master's voice
must have somehow
front-paged the global agenda
during cabinet or committee
or subliminally, its power
to override the smallest
common decencies
approaching the miraculous.

Or perhaps he neither
believes nor disbelieves
the vagrant images
of the policy makers,
but merely accepts
the power given to him
by the easily pimped fears
of a tabloid electorate,
where he learns of its subtleties
in a media haze
of visionary cynicism.

So he scrawls
his coarsely finished stick figures,
chanting exorcisms
from his prehistory
and its fashionable brutality,
while the true cave men,
jiving with Paleolithic
Stone Age chic,
whose own cave paintings,
are a graphic swing band
of primitive sophistication,
must stand appalled.

Like You

Not,
Not like you,
Fierce female gem,
So right,
Yes, so rightly right.

Each tiny bezel
Throws out the correct,
The immaculate answer,
The approved attitude,
Perfectly refracted,
And all with that together
Thing you have.

For you are flawless,
Cut so neat by kin,
By background,
By the right match.

Yet those great and
Deceptive gemsmiths
Will bejewel you
In some Valley of the Kings
And you will adorn,
Without a thought,
Their community,
Waiting for the light.

No, not like you,
No, I'm not.

Midday Walk

Shadow shrunk in ambiguity,
In the suspended course of time,
I walk under an endless sky.
The white heat of day
Is drawn like a billet
From the midday forge
And everywhere, blue draws it
Higher, into the
Colloidal dust of light.

Blue does not press down,
Does not canopy the Earth, for
Blue is the colour of infinity,
The galaxy's heart is blue
And all the stars are nomad
In a blue elixir.
Their language is blue
And each blue thought hurls out
Light year ripples, awaiting,
For ever patient,
The azure reply.

Each one of us walks
Through this blue cloud,
For the skies begin at our feet
And though imprisoned
By the slouching intelligence
Of our past, but one look up
Reveals the behaviour
Of those greater than we.

Muse of Sunsets

Dust, gathering in invisible orbits
Which minutely echo
The huge geometry of Saturn's rings,
Catches the evening spectrum
And toys with, enjoying,
The gentle tides of migration.

As it downfalls in tiny multitudes
On the glass tabletop,
Other floating tribes, reflected back,
Arise and collect vainly
On the upward sky of their universe,
Never to be heard
Through the infinitely holding plane.

Their lighted pinpricks make signals
In that doubly faced firmament
But their communications speed nowhere
And their small, tired cosmos,
Made up of ended things, of aged particles,
Is concluded and made futile
By the whim
Of my Euclidean surface.

Maybe many a civilisation
Has flourished there, on the smalltime
Scales where energy and volume
Approach zero but never meet it,
Maybe they have written
In microscopic chronicles
And catastrophic pinpricks
Of their proud and tragic histories,
Maybe they have tried, too, to colonise
Their universe and have been routed
By the blink of my eye.

Or maybe the muse of sunsets
Has spoken to me,
Her surgery amputating
The discontents of poetry,
Sending into exile
Its posse of magpie squabbling,
Ruling for contentment
And for the repose of maturity,
The fire now burning on leaner fuel.

Neo Con

I deal
Cards I deal
In flurried rings
Ofi-cards
Not Das Kapital
I but lower case i
Cards I deal,
Each one flashing with
Ideal-ism
The ideology
Of dealing.

I deal them out
Staring from my i-space
My ideology space
In the total casino
Of ideology
Flurried imperially
Onto the table
The level playing field.

My byzantine stills
My court card icons
Reassure the players
Gazing with their i-faces
And high stakes regalia
Which hide the knotted lust
Beneath their robes.

And my numbers
Whose values whirr
Beneath their surfaces
Play the big game
While they beget
That strangely figured predator
The square root
Of minus one.

Unreal
I deal

New Jerusalem

She hung high amid the clouds of glory,
For God had specially selected a day
Of crisp winter blue, a high-pressure zone
Of apocalyptic prophecy.
Indifferent to the rules of urban
Planning, the city circled and came down
Immaculately flat and north pointing.
And her dimensions varied Tardis-like,
Her cubic shape reaching fifteen hundred miles
Into the sky, but also twenty-four yards.
Walls of jasper, buildings of glass and gold,
Foundations of uncrushable precious
Stone, twelve gates of pearl (symmetrically dispersed)
Impressed with material wealth the more
Simply minded, perhaps overshadowing
The Tree of Life and the River of Living
Water. This self-glowing city, needing
No light of sun nor moon nor earthly rhythm
Nor any biological nexus,
Absorbed a slow torrent of psalm singing
Faithful but left me pondering upon
Paradise, the holy garden of all
Good things, the day and the night, the beasts and birds
And the naïve absence of cities.

Open Cut

From above, chiselled under the sky
And over the earth,
Gouged in highways of dusty greed,
The grand enormity sprawls.
The bulldozed corpses
Of indigenous cultures,
Ignored and trodden on,
Their music falsely played
And their places, their words,
Their networks of star and time,
Protruding like dead bones.

Unmoved by this upstart geology
Heaven merely observes.
Indifferent to its ancient cause,
That metal-rich hooligan
Whose celestial body blow slowed
Or sped the cataclysmic new day,

And overwritten, curbed and perjured
By the decrees of profit,
The one mantra, the only way,
The thing will remain
Until the indifferent sky
Turns its face to another world,
Where this monument will appear
As nameless and as incomprehensible
As the incurious legions
Of Easter Island.

oral

Sensual media mouth
agape in sexual mastication
grazing like snails
on yielding female fields
with tiny noises of broken
moistures moving among
computer whitened teeth
in a gourmet of sanitised rape.

Minatory media mouth
spattering credo with
scatter-gun militant
enthusiasm gunning down like
injuns the images
of dissent a radio noise of
dogma housed in
pebble-focused eyes devoid
of the pains of doubt.

Infantilised media mouth
of primary colour lips
scarlet garrison to faultless
dentition gym toned wet
roundly opened in perfect
cartoon agile with the
consumerous speech of the
brain stem.

That mainstream mouth now feeds
amid the earth's bounty and
raises a saliva squall
should the feeding flicker.

With fistfuls of warrior
sperm whole rafts
of first-world eggs can be
fertilised
every one a fifty-fold disaster
for each aperture consumes
half
a hundred.

Parallel Rider

I'm sure he's a horseman
Who rides abreast of me,
Strangely signing to pull over
Yet keeping easy pace
As the gums surge past
My open window.
His scattered cantering
And lopsided gallops,
Seemingly windswept of purpose,
Call from another world.

He pleads, he beckons,
He halloos and hallays,
His cluttered mass of equipment
Forming random haloes
Of yet unbegun purpose.
His oddly angled semaphores
Disregard all matters
Of road safety as he cajoles
His steed to easily
Surpass my vehicle.

He comes from the other life,
The full moon of imagination
And the high noon of the child
Who can change saddles
With a hundred other lives.

He's the grand summoner of dreams,
His own road map,
Intimately parallel
To this fully minded world
And a permanent reproof
To that *achtung minen*
Of prudence.

Looking for the bends ahead.,
I judiciously close up on him.

Plato's Horses – from *Phaedrus*

One chariot, and
Two trotting horses lead the way
Upward to the One,
To the sun of all truth
Ineffably glowing
On the horizon.

One ego's lash impels
Them both, one black
And lathered with passion,
Often refusing, tossing
Her head, eyes round
With a primitive fear
Of the fiery star,
While the other horse,
White and disciplined,
Feels no whip
And no contradictions disturb
His flight, reason's clinical blade,
Abounding with a miser's eye
The measurement of the senses.

Wayward, moody and
Illogical, one beast shows no
Inclination for the noble
Path, no leaning towards
The cool tyranny of the Absolute.

The other is agreeable,
Complaisant and utters
The milk of rationality
As the road streams past.

Yet one absolute's
As good as any other, only
Differing in the pyramids
Of the tortured.

And the pale horse knows
The whereabouts
Of the killing fields.

Psychotoxic

She weaves judgemental among the crystal
Fringes of yourself, that you whose fabric
Holds a multifold of feathered sinews.

She fingers, quite by chance, the delicate
Arches of light, whose strength upholds the day's
Frontiers of dream and of comprehension.

Caressing each plane and pristine face, she,
Gourmand for your innocent brightness, with
Unhurried calculation, bares her smiles,

And, quite unbidden, after due recourse
To the civilities of hatred, the
Rough thrust of her spite makes a laceration,

And with sensual abrasion rubs raw
The pain with sympathy, or the unsaid
Reproach, or with the prolonged riptide of her gaze.

Raku

It's the pottery of simple delight
Because it's devoid of false refinement
And not good food for
The intellectually prominent.

A rough clay is used,
Full of grit and irregularities
To remind us of the virtues
Of the unmanufactured artefact.

Fired to feel like biscuit,
The pot is dipped in glaze,
A kind of creamy powdered glass,
And then fired again until,
On inspection, it takes on
The glossy appearance of ice.

Plucked from the kiln
With tongs of iron, the vessel
Is placed among leaves
Which catch fire and burn away
In a carbon-rich atmosphere,
Thus changing the glaze qualities.
And then, in a final touch
Of buoyant enthusiasm,
The still hot piece is immersed
In water.

Simple pleasure it is,
But not without a book length
Of highly retentive learning
And calculation, a process so opposite
To the joys of Raku,
It is almost a pleasure
In itself.

Reliquary

Little Soso, little Joe,
Who took the seditious title
Of Koba, a Georgian Ned Kelly
And at the apex
Of the Revolution
Transformed his name
Through the blast furnace
Into Stalin, the Russian Man of Steel,
Denied the names
Of much frailer creatures,
Their flesh as remote from his metal
As hearth is from holocaust.

Perhaps he used the Gulags' bones
As a logical foundation
For the resurgent steel
Of Russian industry
And the bones, too,
Of the masses casually executed,
Their calcium, we can suppose,
Making the concrete strong
And purging
From the world's sight
Not with a whispered gesture,
But with a coal-fired fist,
All the evidence
That could be assembled.
They could not reproach,

Cross examine or hold up
To ridicule the tyrant's
Rational purposes,
Since not even a pile of ash
Would remain.

But somewhere in the Kremlin,
Embalmed like a wax candle,
He lingers, whose name sits
Like a continent
And whose relics will one day
Call forth miracles.

Snake

Stumbling along a cliff
To view the lighthouse
Off Corny Point,
I stumble instead
Upon a snake,
Brown, coiled up
Basking, complacently
Immune from all predation.

There is the presence
Of an eye
Deep within
Its nondescript colour
Which returns my look,
Assuming a baleful patience
Such that might have viewed
The laying down
Of ancient continents.

Though it resembles
Not much more
Than a newly laid
Pile of ordure,
Neither diamond sleek,
Reflective nor sinuous,
I have a sudden respect
For this member
Of an archaic society.

Despite my position
At the apex
Of evolution,
I falter
And pick the path
Of least venomosity,
My mortality seeming
Slight and hurried
As this creature,
Resonant
With the knowledge
Inside the rocks
And of the ancient skies,
Proclaims its symbolic power
Like Medusa.

Soccer Balls

This,
rolls to a stop,
a tombstone halt
but weaving still the magic
that gave pause
to Rommel's 88s.

That,
racing along,
busied with the clan gossip,
like Hermes
bearing tales from Olympus,
slows down
to rub a confiding shoulder
with one in the know.

Others,
quietly browsing in herds,
seeking deliberately the mud,
the gothic melancholy
of the outsider,
sit like mushrooms,
like sudden beads of light.

They,
nightly gathered
in the net bags,
conduct their silent orgies
and breed no offspring
but the allurement
which,
in the next morning,
stalls the day
of every young one.

Supermen

I, for the honour of the Achaeans,
Faced the warlike courage
Of those in Ilium,
Where I once stood
Among the living before Troy
And did not see the bright
Trojan spearhead
Guided by the hand of Ares
But felt it bite through the leather
And spill my entrails in the dust.
I sank into the hateful darkness,
Torn by the bronze,
And though I sent many
To the shadowy realm,
Still I lay,
Waiting to be received
By those in the Elysian Fields.

I, for the love of Queen Marie,
Lay broken at Naseby,
Where we stood
Like a wall of brass
Against the skill of their cavalry.
I did not see the bright Puritan sword
Where Cromwell's troopers dispatched
The last valour of Rupert's Bluecoats,
I lay ruined among the skipping shot
And did not see
But the broad moor
So close to my eye
And the day's harvest
At the Gates of Paradise.

I, for the Son of Heaven,
Prepared for the invader,
To defy his ambitions,
To yield up my wholehearted life,
But I did not see the single aircraft
In our undefended skies,
Nor its inexplicable course.
I did not see the light,
So fast did it tear us down,
Nor the bent column
Whose shadowy head
Drew all things upward
Into its brilliance.
Still I lay entombed in silhouette
Awaiting my rebirth.

I, for the honour of Krypton,
Faced the evil courage
Of those lawbreakers
And did not see the bright bullets
Spat out by Lex Luthor himself,
Nor feel them bite through
My invulnerable skin,
Because my chest
Kablammed them back
Where they belonged,
As I stood among
The ruins of all their plans,
My six-pack barely raising a dust.

Only kryptonite
Can lay me low,
And not even
The thermonuclear option,
With all their hallelujahs
Will take me down.

The Elite

They deride the popular voice and have
Forced into the world a grip as profound
As Diocletian's and move empires of words
To rule a ditch, or dispel sovereignty
With uncontested cant. They inhabit
The Ruler's mind, and, anticipating,
They input, with careful nurturing grains
Of rational illumination, then,
Withdrawn, they magnify the catechism
Of procedures, wherein they gain potency.
In the passage of information they
Dance like feelered insects in codes assured;
In the dispensation of policy,
They regretfully minister to the
Needful application of coercion.

Their penned-in world's most real, for each stroke, each
Sign, contains a Universe (upon which
The flesh sunders) of categories – their
Lumbering denser-than-air machine alights
On clouds and wafts somewhere on tufts of time,
Grazing on reality, then departs,
Despoiling as the goat, as the cloven hoof,
The permanent fondness of nature for
The eccentric, the fragile, the obscure.

Time

Tedious master of my maturity
Were you, time, and yet these eyes
Have watched you alter. A year of your body

Was once incomprehensible and comprised
Days gigantically adrift.
You were my pedantic text, though paradise

To elders who themselves longed for the gift
Of your earlier largesse.
In my impatience, heedless of any thrift,

I bankrolled whatever wonderful request
The universe made of me,
Laying up no treasure, not seeing your jest.

In your vast present, I played upon the white beach
Of the imagination,
The cataract's far thunder, where the skies meet

Oblivion, no great thing. No submission
Would be conceded to death,
Whose structure was beyond my young reason.

But like the pause between every breath,
Your assassin in ambush
Awaits your command to submerge this doomed flesh

Beneath your rising waters; that one small push
Will extinguish all my world
And drown my final light in its blinding rush.

Yet like two struggling birds in forgetfulness
Of their flight, both death and time
Will tumble in the dissolution of my strength.

For death with his braggadocio design
Is but the symmetry of time,
And both less than that mortality whose life
Gave them breath.

Too Lazy

Fat rolls of sleep,
Those dozing sumos,
Ripple with gelatinous sloth
Through my pond.

All the sun's bright day,
Its lyric of flowering clouds
And suggestive breeze
Knock in vain at my window.

And yes, yes,
I know the mystic appeal
Of transparent layers of wonder
And perfumed foliage
And the horizon's repose
On the distant sky.

I know, too, the birdsong
Of some rapid act
Of lust
And the sudden noise
Of small carnivores
And their prey
In the spring laden
Cosmic wheel
Of life and death.

But I say no,
And my barely articulate
Homo Sapiens Sapiens body,
Refuses the walk.
It says no too.

Trance

Ten minutes of ticktocktime,
I needed just that
To open a small-scale trance,
A release from the sudden imposition
Of needs,
A small-scale trance
To remind
And refresh with its sanctuary
The inviolate period
Of reflection,
Of cave-old thought.

Voyagers in the Tea Tree Gully Library

To the quiet sedation
of the air conditioner
the coffee rings descend
unwillingly into the black cup –
to the chink of cutlery
and the hissing whoosh
of the percolator
the lotus eaters continue
their quest for refreshment.

Voices ask for purpose,
sing to make sense and reason
and question marks metallically flit
among the seekers,
an older voice drifting behind,
while a higher register,
contrapunto,
gives away Athene in disguise.

And looking outside
to the square-rigged sunlight
among the ton-heavy trees
and their fingerlings of shade,
they see the four winds play
in shadow where the day stands up
like the oars
of the hollow ships.

The scrub of biro on page
presses deeply
and they still scrawl
to that little thing of a heartbeat,
as the blue beaked nib squinting
through their fingers
flows and makes its sound,
a heated stake
to plunge into the single eye
of ignorance.

And among the smell of books
riffling in virgin pages,
the tip tap keyboards
peck busily on an odyssey
of learning
where you may never arrive.

And in the high noon of youth
amid other libraries
as remote as Ithaca,
we too were silent
on a peak in Darien.

Willow

Godddess of the willow,
Tree of enchantment,
Ancient tree of waters,
Of the Moon that owns them,
Tree of willow words,
Wicker, Salix, Osier,
Tree of witchcraft and wise women,
Tree of wicked wiccan spells,
Charms of knowing, allaying
And preservation,
You it is,
Who with your drooping hair
Speaks to me in your
Forbidden siren song,
Seducing me and overwriting
My sad little mortal chipset '
Through your strident media.

So I must consume
Your sacred imagery,
And lavish myself
In your excess, greed,
Your sexual surfeit
And expire, degenerate
In your whispering cavern.

And I will join the other poets,
Wailing at the River Styx,
That even the ever-renewing virgin
Gave in to overwhelming
Economic pressure
In the service of the market economy,
And made herself a corporate tart,
Selling tickets for Madonna.

Winter Black

Remote from the sun's tantrums,
Underneath the soil's
Frail veneer of fertility,
The heart of the earth
Goes about its way
Abounding in blackness
In the beloved winter,
Most fruitful of seasons.

That blind wisdom
Constructs the next year's growth,
Adapts to the ever-bending earth
And sways oh so lugubriously
To the gravitational nodes which
Cruise through the planet's body.

The taproots grip and claw
The subterrene matter,
To add the strength
Of centuries to their positions
In the biosphere,
To realise their wisdom
With lightless knowledge
And to keep safe the life.

Another pendulum
Prevails here, whose period
Swings to the spread of continents
And to the extinction of species,
Its blackness laughing
At the blurring solar tracks,
At the puffings of the moon
And the wobbling stars.

It has given us the grasses,
Their silken harvests,
The suite of necessary animals,
And on some other underground day
It might confer its bounty
To other creatures
Perhaps less close
To the busy sun.

Witchcraft

Their anxiety is a witchcraft
derived from the bleak spirit
of their old villages,
shadowed by priest,
bailiff and moneylender
and the impossible wagonload
of superstition,
staring back with the evil eye
on every thought,
every aspiration.

Their anxiety is a witchcraft,
where they mimic the fear
in order to disarm it,
to parry the malice of the skies,
whose choreography
of cracking quarterstaff blows
they fend off
with the constant practice
of their weaponry,
their rehearsal of ill luck.

And still they rehearse
their witchcraft of anxiety,
to keep safe the hearth
and its family fortunes
but where once they fell soft
and the enemy fell hard,
they now stumble
with such force,
that their enemy
need hardly trip at all.

And such is the conjuring
of their modern enchantments
that, in repeating
all his malice,
they embody once more
in their never-ending rituals,
the preying fears
derived from the bleak heart
of their ancient homes.

www.ingramcontent.com/pod-product-compliance
Lightning Source LLC
Chambersburg PA
CBHW062146100526
44589CB00014B/1711